EARTH CARE
Don't Trash This Planet

Karolyn Kendrick

A Harcourt Achieve Imprint

www.Steck-Vaughn.com
1-800-531-5015

Earth Care: Don't Trash This Planet
By Karolyn Kendrick

Photo Acknowledgements
Cover ©Mitsuaki Iwago/Minden Pictures; P. 7 ©Louie Psihoyos/CORBIS; p. 12 ©Mike Farruggia; p. 15 ©Bill Ross/CORBIS; p. 17 ©Larry Lee Photography/CORBIS; p. 18 ©Chinch Gryniewicz; Ecoscene/CORBIS; p. 23 ©David Butow/CORBIS SABA; p. 26–27 ©Pete Atkinson/Getty Images; p. 28 photo courtesy of the Campus Center for Appropriate Technology, a Program of Associated Students of Humboldt State University.

Additional photography by BrandX Royalty Free; Digital Vision/Getty Royalty Free; Photodisc/Getty Royalty Free; Royalty-Free/CORBIS.

ISBN 1-4190-2279-2

© 2007 Harcourt Achieve Inc.
All rights reserved. No part of the material protected by this copyright may be reproduced or utilized in any form or by any means, in whole or in part, without permission in writing from the copyright owner. Requests for permission should be mailed to: Paralegal Department, 6277 Sea Harbor Drive, Orlando, FL 32887.

Steck-Vaughn is a trademark of Harcourt Achieve Inc.

Printed in the United States of America
1 2 3 4 5 6 7 8 152 12 11 10 09 08 07 06 05

Table of Contents

Introduction
It's Your Planet 4

Chapter 1
Solid Waste: The Garbage Go-Round 6
    The Dump Artists 12

Chapter 2
Fossil Fuels: Using Up the Earth 14
    Make a Wind Gauge 20

Chapter 3
Global Warming: Who Turned Up the Heat? 22
    Do-It-Yourself Power 28

Glossary 30

Index 32

Introduction

It's Your Planet

Think about how you start an average morning. Your alarm goes off. You turn on a light. You take a hot shower. You put on clean clothes. You empty a carton of milk and throw it out. Someone drives you to school.

It takes a lot of energy and lots of **natural resources** just to start your day. The alarm clock and the light both use electricity. The electricity probably comes from power plants that burn coal or oil. The coal or oil must be taken from the earth and processed. Processing oil requires machines that use more energy. Burning oil and coal pollutes the air. The detergent from your laundry drains into the ground and possibly the water supply. It goes on and on.

Earth is our home. It's the only one we've got. Our decisions and actions have an impact on the land, water, and air. How can we use our planet's resources without trashing the planet? You'll find some answers in this book.

Chapter 1

Solid Waste: The Garbage Go-Round

You stop at the store for a snack. You tear off the wrapper. What do you do with it? Most people just throw it away. After a while, those wrappers add up.

Imagine this. Stack 30 students onto a giant scale. They'd weigh about 1,180 kilograms (2,600 pounds). That's how much garbage the average person makes every year. It's not just wrappers, either. It's everything from banana peels to batteries.

Now, multiply that by all the people in the United States. That would make more than 336 million metric tons (370 million tons) of trash each year. Can you picture that? It's about the weight of 67 million full-grown African elephants.

Where does all that trash go? Well, old glass, plastic, and paper can be used to make new products. In the U.S., only about 27 percent gets **recycled**, though. (See page 11.) Another 17 percent is burned to make electricity. Good idea, right? Yet, burning garbage gives off **toxic** gases. So, it's not a perfect solution.

What happens to the rest of our trash? It gets dumped into one of our 1,700 landfills.

Basically, a landfill is a giant pile of trash. It has strong plastic liners on the sides and bottom. The liners protect the soil and groundwater below.

Most of the garbage in a landfill will rot, over time. Rotting is caused by tiny **bacteria** and **fungi**. They eat anything that was once alive, such as old food, paper, and wood. If you've ever smelled spoiled meat or seen moldy bread, you've seen rotting in action. When garbage has **decomposed** all the way, it becomes part of the soil.

Fresh Kills landfill collects New York City's garbage. It's so big that astronauts can see it from space.

Unfortunately, decomposing trash takes a long time to go away. A newspaper, for instance, can take 40 years to break down. Some trash takes even longer. Metal breaks down very slowly. Glass can hang around for a million years. Some plastics will never break down. They are not **biodegradable**.

Water pollution is another problem. When rain falls on a landfill, it soaks into the rotting garbage. The rainwater makes a soup of bacteria and chemicals. This soup is called leachate. If there is a rip in the landfill's plastic liner, the leachate gets out. It leaks into streams or groundwater. Leachate is **hazardous**. It can make animals and people sick.

Landfills also pollute the air. As bacteria eat the garbage, they give off gases called carbon dioxide and methane. (See Chapter 3.) The gases are dangerous to breathe. Plus, methane is **flammable**. If it builds up, it could cause an explosion. Landfills use pipes to remove it safely. Some landfills recycle the methane. It can be burned to heat houses or make electricity.

Recycling a Landfill

When a landfill is full, it closes down. So, what happens to the smelly mountain of garbage? Some communities recycle their landfills. They turn the garbage heaps into parks and golf courses.

How a Landfill Works

What happens at a landfill?

1. Giant bulldozers rumble over each day's garbage. They pack it into tight cells. Then, they cover it with dirt.

2. Under the ground, bacteria do their work. They break down the garbage.

3. Liners protect the soil and groundwater.

4. Leachate pipes collect liquid waste.

5. Gas pipes collect methane. In some landfills, methane is pumped to power plants. There it's turned into electricity.

6. Meanwhile, special **monitors** check the groundwater and air for leaks.

Turning a landfill into something else is not always easy. Just ask the golfers at the Englewood Golf Course in Colorado. They've found bowling balls and tires on the greens. That's because landfills sink as the garbage rots. Trash that hasn't broken down rises to the surface.

Methane is an even bigger problem. At a park in Charlotte, North Carolina, a mom chased a soccer ball into a hole. She lit a lighter to see better. KABOOM! Methane gas from the landfill exploded. Luckily, no one was seriously hurt.

New York City has the toughest job of all. Officials there want to recycle the world's biggest landfill. The Fresh Kills landfill sits on Staten Island. It's so big that astronauts can see it from space. Four giant trash hills rise 27 to 69 meters (90 to 225 feet) into the air.

Brian Goldberg came up with a plan for Fresh Kills. He says the project will take 30 years. When it's done, the trash hills will be a park. New Yorkers will go canoeing, hiking, and mountain biking there. It will have restaurants and outdoor markets. Not only that, methane from the decomposing garbage will heat 25,000 homes. That's not such a bad fate for your snack wrapper.

What's in Your Garbage?

U.S. Waste, 2001 (source: U.S. Environmental Protection Agency)

This photo shows some of the things in landfills. With a little effort, we could keep many items from getting there in the first place. Here's how:

Reuse. Think up new ways to use old stuff. Make a CD shelf from shoeboxes. Sew a pillow out of an old t-shirt. Be creative.

Recycle. Follow your community's rules for recycling. It's the law. **Organize** a drive to collect items and take them to recycling plants. You can raise money for a good cause.

Compost. Some people keep a compost heap in their garden. **Compost** can be made from animal wastes and anything made from plants. Food scraps can also be composted. Composted waste eventually turns into soil. Composting reduces trash and makes soil better for planting.

- Rubber, Leather, and Textiles 7.1%
- Glass 5.5%
- Wood 5.7%
- Other 3.4%
- Paper 35.7%
- Yard Trimmings 12.2%
- Food Scraps 11.4%
- Plastics 11.1%
- Metal 7.9%

The Dump Artists

In the spring of 2005, raiding the dump was Mike's job. Mike Farruggia was the official artist-in-residence at the San Francisco landfill. Every three months, a new artist works the landfill. Norcal Waste Systems runs the art program there.

"I had heard of the 3 Rs," says Mike. "Reduce, Reuse, Recycle. The dump has a fourth: Rot (for composting). I added a fifth: Repair!"

Often, broken things can be fixed, Mike says. They don't have to be thrown away. A bike may just need a small repair. Maybe a piece of furniture needs some glue. "In other parts of the world, every plastic bag and scrap of wood has value," he says.

Mike likes to make new things out of old trash. "You find a pair of crutches. You think, what can I make? Maybe a bookshelf." Old game tiles became the numbers on a clock.

There's a quiet hill above the noisy dump. On it, the dump artists have made a sculpture garden. Everything there is made from garbage. It's a place where an old toilet seat could become part of a masterpiece.

Mike built this scooter from parts he found at the dump.

Chapter 2

Fossil Fuels: Using Up the Earth

The world depends on **fossil fuels** to produce energy. Fossil fuels include oil, natural gas, and coal. Power plants burn them to make electricity. The cars and planes we travel in burn fuel made from oil. The same resources heat and cool our homes, schools, and offices. In fact, 85 percent of our energy comes from fossil fuels. Some even help us grow our food. They are used to make **fertilizer**.

The United States is the world's biggest consumer of fossil fuels. Americans make up less than five percent of the world's population. Yet, they use more than 25 percent of the world's fossil fuels. In a day, the average American uses almost three gallons of oil. People in other countries tend to use less fossil fuels. In Mexico, for example, each person uses only two-thirds of a gallon of oil a day.

So, how does our fossil fuel habit affect the planet? It pollutes the air, for one. When fossil fuels burn, they give off gases. One of those gases is carbon dioxide.

Levels of carbon dioxide in the air are increasing. They may be changing the climate on Earth. (See Chapter 3.)

Fossil fuels also give off nitrogen oxides and sulfur oxides. These gases can harm the environment in two ways. They react with sunlight to form **ozone** gas. This can be bad for your eyes and lungs. Also, oxides mix with water in the air to form acids. The acids fall back to Earth when it rains. "Acid rain" can kill fish. It can also damage plants and trees.

The United States uses about 20 million barrels of oil each day. That's four times more than any other country on the planet.

Fossil fuels are also disappearing fast. They are called *nonrenewable* resources because we can't make more. Once we use them up, they're gone.

Here's why. Oil and coal are made from old organic material. Organic material is anything that was once alive. Millions of years ago, plants and animals died and were buried under layers of dirt. They began to rot. Pressure and heat packed the rotting material down. Eventually, the mixture changed into fossil fuels.

This process took millions of years. That's much too slow to replace what we use. Every year, the world burns fossil fuels at a faster rate. That rate has doubled every 20 years since 1900.

When will fossil fuels run out? No one really knows. Half of the planet's supply may be gone already. Some experts think we may run out of oil by 2050.

Looking to the Sun

What will we use for energy when all the fossil fuel is gone? Scientists are **investigating** renewable energy sources. A renewable source never runs out. The sun and the wind are the best examples. They currently provide the most useful renewable sources of energy.

Solar energy can be collected from the sun in two ways. One is passive. The other is active. Passive solar energy is collected in the place where it's needed. Sit by a sunny window on a cold day. You'll feel the heat from passive solar energy at work. Entire buildings can

Since 1900, energy use has increased rapidly. Before the 1800s, most power was provided by humans, animals, fire, and the sun.

be heated this way. As the sun crosses the sky, windows facing it take in more of the sun's rays. Builders add tiles to store heat inside the building. Dark colors work best. They **absorb** the solar energy. Light colors **reflect** the sun's rays.

Solar panels use the sun's rays to heat a house.

Active solar technology uses machines to move that energy around. Here's an example. The sun heats panels on the roof. Under the panels are pipes filled with water. When the panels heat up, the water heats up, too. Pumps push the water throughout the building.

Solar cells are another kind of active solar technology. They change sunlight into electricity. Solar cells have many uses. They can even power car engines. Every two years, drivers gather for the North American Solar Challenge in Austin, Texas. They race to Calgary, Canada, in sleek "sunraycers." The cars can travel up to 100 miles per hour. The technology still needs work, though. Solar cells don't store much power. When the sun goes down, the race stops for the day.

Wind is another renewable energy source. Wind power is growing around the world. Giant windmills churn on old farmland and on mountaintops. Their design is simple. Wind turns the blades of a giant fan. The fan is called a **turbine**. The turbine operates a **generator**. The generator turns the mechanical energy of the turbine into electricity. Windmills now power about 1.6 million homes in the United States.

Sun and wind technology has a long way to go. Still, these two sources may produce most of our energy in the future. Turn on your lights in the year 2050. You might have the sun and the wind to thank.

Wind turbines turn wind energy into electricity.

Make a Wind Gauge

Materials
- five, three-ounce paper cups
- paper punch
- ruler
- two straws
- straight pin
- scissors
- stapler
- sharp pencil with an eraser

How much energy can the wind create? It depends on the wind speed. Scientists measure wind speed with an **anemometer,** or wind gauge. Follow these directions and make your own.

1. Take four of the cups. Punch a hole ½ inch below the rim of each.

2. Push a straw through the hole of one cup. Fold the end of the straw. Staple it to the inside of the cup across from the hole. Repeat this for a second cup.

3. Take the fifth cup. Punch four equally spaced holes a ¼ inch below the rim. Then punch a hole in the center of the bottom of the cup.

4. Take one cup-and-straw pair. Slide the free end of the straw through two opposite holes of the fifth cup. Take a one-holed cup without a straw. Slide it onto the free end of the straw. Bend the straw. Staple it to the inside of the cup.

5. Repeat step 4 with the remaining cups. The open ends of the cups should face the same direction around the center cup.

6. Push the straight pin through the two straws where they meet.

7. Put the eraser end of the pencil through the bottom hole in the center cup. Push the pin into the eraser. Your wind gauge is ready to use.

8. Measure the distance around the cups. Hold a string around the outside of the cups. Mark the place where one end meets the other. Lay the string straight. Measure it with the ruler. This is the **circumference**.

9. Mark one of the cups to use as a counter. Count the number of times the marked cup goes around in one minute. These are your revolutions per minute (RPM). Multiply the RPM by the circumference. That's the speed of the wind per minute.

Chapter 3

Global Warming: Who Turned Up the Heat?

In Los Angeles, California, thousands of cars sit in traffic every day. In Alaska, polar bears are struggling to find food. What do these two things have to do with each other? Maybe everything. If that seems strange, keep reading.

During the winter, large areas of Arctic seawater freeze. Polar bears spend months on the sea ice hunting seals. When the ice melts, the bears go ashore. Food becomes harder to find. The bears eat eggs, birds, even garbage. When the sea freezes again, they go back to hunting seals.

In recent years, sea ice has been melting earlier and earlier. The bears must go ashore sooner. They have less to eat. Many of them are losing weight. They're giving birth to fewer cubs. Some bears get stuck as the sea ice breaks up around them. It's tragic. Why is this happening to them?

Scientists are worried about the polar bears. Yet the bears may be a sign of a much bigger problem. That problem is global climate change.

Little by little, the average temperature of our planet is rising. Huge masses of ice called **glaciers** are shrinking. Antarctic ice sheets are melting. Frozen ground called **tundra** is thawing. As more ice melts, the temperature of the air and oceans is increasing.

Climate change is nothing new for the planet. Over millions of years, Earth warms and cools naturally. The last "ice age" ended just 12,000 years ago. Before then, ice covered much of North America all year round.

This time, though, human beings may be the cause. We're burning too many fossil fuels. That's where those Los Angeles traffic jams come in.

What does a traffic jam have to do with a hungry polar bear?

Now think back to what you know about fossil fuels. Cars burn fossil fuels. So do power plants. When the fuels burn, gases are produced. These gases rise into the air. There, they blanket Earth's atmosphere with pollution. This causes the "greenhouse effect."

How does the greenhouse effect work? The sun heats our planet during the day. The oceans and the ground absorb the energy. At night, they radiate that heat back into the air. Some of the heat escapes back into space. The rest gets trapped in the polluted **atmosphere**. Greenhouse gases, like carbon dioxide and methane, help trap the heat.

The Greenhouse Effect

1. The sun's rays pass through the earth's atmosphere.
2. Solar radiation heats the ground and the oceans.
3. Heat rises from the earth and seas back into the atmosphere.
4. Some heat escapes into space.
5. Some heat is trapped inside Earth's atmosphere by greenhouse gases.
6. Earth's average temperature rises, thawing polar ice.

Some of the greenhouse gases are there naturally. Without them, all the heat from the sun would escape into space. The earth would be too cold to support life.

So, what's the problem? Since the 1800s, more and more greenhouse gases are pumped into the air. The level of carbon dioxide has increased by one-third in the last 250 years. Methane levels have more than doubled. These gases trap more heat each year. Little by little, the blanket of pollution gets thicker. The planet gets warmer. What will happen if things continue to heat up?

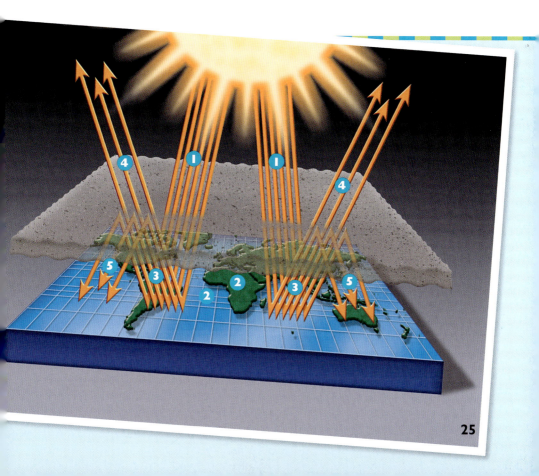

The Heat is On

No one knows exactly how global warming will ultimately change the earth. Scientists disagree about how bad the problem is. Still, many of them share some big concerns. First of all, ocean levels are rising. As Earth gets warmer, ice is melting in the polar regions. Water from the melted ice pours into the ocean. Rising air temperatures heat the water even more. Water expands when it gets warm. The result is an increasing amount of ocean water. In the future, the oceans could cover low-lying islands. Coastal areas might flood. Imagine New York City completely underwater.

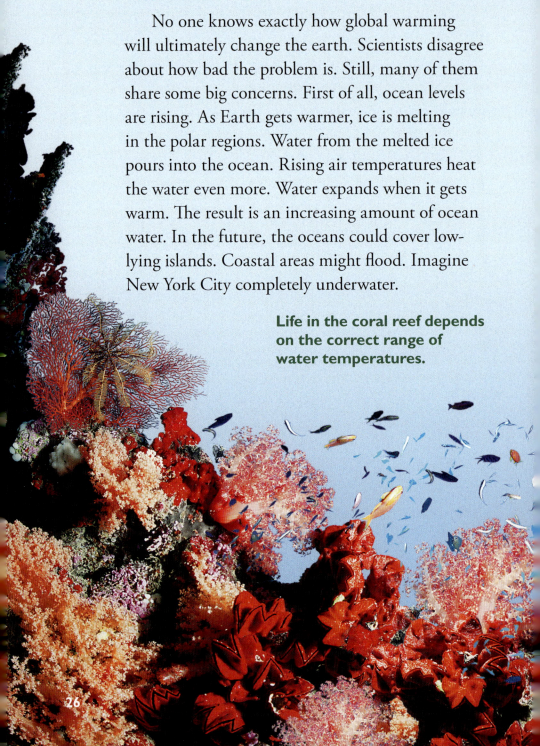

Life in the coral reef depends on the correct range of water temperatures.

Global warming also makes life difficult for some animal species. Many animals depend on plants for food. Plants grow at certain temperature ranges. As temperatures change, some plants will die off. Animals will need new sources of food. Some will be forced to **migrate**. Animals that can't adapt may die out and become **extinct**.

Sea life is affected, too. About one-fourth of all marine animals and plants live on coral reefs. Reefs are like cities in the sea. They shelter thousands of sponges, crabs, shrimp, and other creatures. Many larger fish and sea mammals depend on them for food. However, coral is very sensitive to water temperature. When temperatures rise too high, the coral dies. Many of the creatures that live in the coral reefs die, as well.

People are starting to think about these problems. World leaders meet regularly to discuss global warming. Many of them have agreed to cut back on fossil fuels. Will it be enough? No one knows.

Do-It-Yourself Power

Welcome to Eco-House. It's part of Humboldt State University in Arcata, California. Eco-House was set up in 1978. Its purpose is to show how we can live without using up Earth's nonrenewable resources. Every year, three new students move in. Dozens more volunteer to help out with projects.

Eco-House runs on renewable energy. Solar cells on the roof collect the sun's rays. They produce electricity from the energy. A wind turbine by the door generates more electricity. The house also has a generator that burns used cooking oil from the school cafeteria.

"It's exciting to live here!" says Glenn Howe. "Everyone cares so much about what they do."

Glenn wasn't always an **environmentalist**. "When I was in middle school, I just complained," he says. "I had no idea that my actions could make a difference." Now Glenn is living in Eco-House. If he wants to watch TV, he has to pedal. His legwork powers a generator. This makes enough electricity to run the TV. All the **appliances** in the house can run on human power, too.

How can you help the planet? Glenn has some tips.

- Ride your bike or walk. "It makes a big difference in our energy use," says Glenn.
- Put caulk and weather-stripping around windows and doors in your home. They keep heat in and conserve energy.
- Turn off appliances when they're not in use.

Glossary

absorb (*verb*) to take in or soak up

anemometer (*noun*) a tool that measures wind speed

appliance (*noun*) a machine that does a particular job in a house

atmosphere (*noun*) the layer of gases that surround a planet

bacteria (*noun*) tiny organisms that feed on organic matter

biodegradable (*adjective*) able to decay and be absorbed by the environment

circumference (*noun*) the distance around the outside of a circle

compost (*noun*) the soil formed from decaying plant or animal material

decompose (*verb*) to rot or decay naturally

environmentalist (*noun*) someone who is concerned about the health of the planet

extinct (*adjective*) no longer living

fertilizer (*noun*) a substance that helps plants grow

flammable (*adjective*) easy to burn

fossil fuel (*noun*) coal, oil, or natural gas formed from decayed animals and plants

fungi (*noun*) plural of fungus; plantlike organisms that help break down organic matter

generator (*noun*) a machine that changes mechanical energy into electricity

glacier (*noun*) a huge mass of ice

hazardous (*adjective*) dangerous

impact (*noun*) the effect one thing has on something else

investigate (*verb*) to look into; to find information

migrate (*verb*) to move from one region to another

monitor (*noun*) a tool that measures or keeps track of something

natural resource (*noun*) a valuable supply of energy, food, or materials from Earth

organize (*verb*) to plan something; to put together in an orderly way

ozone (*noun*) a gas formed from oxygen that can be harmful to breathe

reflect (*verb*) to bounce back

recycle (*verb*) to turn used material into new things

toxic (*adjective*) poisonous

tundra (*noun*) an area in the Artic where the ground is permanently frozen

turbine (*noun*) an engine that runs when water, air, or steam turns the blades of a wheel

Idioms

not such a bad fate (*page 10*) not the worst result
Switching to solar energy is not such a bad fate.

Index

anemometers, 20–21
art, 13
atmosphere, 24

bacteria, 7, 8, 9

carbon dioxide, 8, 14–15, 24–25
climate changes, 15, 22–27
compost, 11
coral reefs, 26–27

decomposing trash, 7–8

Eco-House, 29
electricity, 5, 6, 9, 14, 18, 19, 29

Farruggia, Mike, 13
fossil fuels, 14–16, 23–24, 27

garbage, 6–11
generators, 19, 29
global warming, 22–27
greenhouse effect, 24–25

landfills, 7, 8, 9, 10, 11, 13
leachate, 8, 9

methane, 8, 9, 10, 25

natural resources, 5
nonrenewable resources, 16, 29

ocean levels, 26
ozone gas, 15

pollution, 5, 8, 14, 24, 25
power plants, 5, 9, 14, 24

recycling, 6, 8, 10, 11, 13
renewable resources, 16, 19, 29
reuse, 11, 13

solar cells, 18, 29
solar energy, 16–18, 19, 29

wind energy, 16, 19, 20, 29
wind gauges, 20–21
wind turbines, 19, 29